All About Your Kitten

Contents

Cats have lived side by side with man for at least 4,000 years. Originally, their presence was encouraged by the Ancient Egyptians, who had developed the skills necessary for farming, but needed assistance in controlling the vast numbers of vermin that pillaged their grain stores.

The fact that cats were originally domesticated for their hunting skills should be remembered by any owner who is shocked when their gentle companion is discovered killing birds and rodents. Cats were so important to the Egyptians that they were eventually worshipped as gods.

The fortunes of the cat have gone through good times and bad – they were tortured and killed due to their suspected association with witches in Europe in the Middle Ages. But, nowadays, the cat is our number one, most popular pet.

The cat is now our most popular pet.

The Adaptable Cat

The cat's popularity is well deserved, as it fits in perfectly with our modern lifestyle. Cats living in urban areas are best kept indoors, but suburban and rural cats can enjoy the freedom to roam. With both parents in many families going out to work during the day, a cat, or better still, two cats, can reasonably be left to their own devices for several hours at a time, whereas dogs need much more human companionship. Of course, a young kitten, or a cat that is confined indoors, will be more reliant upon its owners than an adult cat that has the use of a cat-flap.

Responsibilities

Despite their relative independence, taking responsibility for any living creature is not something that should be done lightly. Before taking on a cat, you should consider if you have the time, the patience and the money to care for it properly. The cost of feeding a cat is not great, but you must also be able to provide care when you are away, and the cost of veterinary treatment, both for preventative care and for when things go wrong.

Best of friends: The Owl and the Pussycat.

3

Introduction

Life-span

The owner of a new kitten can realistically hope that their new pet will live for fifteen or sixteen years. For a family with young children, this means that the cat will live alongside them until the kids grow into adults, and perhaps even after they leave home. Many hefty tomes have been written about the care of cats throughout their life, but this book is aimed as a basic guide for the owner of a new kitten, and as such, will concentrate upon its care and development during those early months.

Kittens are irresistible, but you must be prepared to care for your cat throughout its life.

Finding A Kitten

The first decision you will need to take is whether you want a pedigree kitten or whether you will be perfectly happy with a non-pedigree cat. If you fancy a highly-bred specimen, you will need to find a reputable breeder. Your veterinary surgeon may be able to point you in the right direction locally, you could look in one of the many cat magazines that can be purchased nowadays, or you can contact one of the Cat Fancy associations.

The choice of pedigree is very much one of personal preference – it may well be that the characteristics of one particular breed appeal to you. However, it is important to bear in mind that, just like finely-tuned sports cars, pedigree cats do require that little extra bit of care and attention, and will probably be more costly to 'run', as well as taking on board the initial purchase price.

The majority of owners opt for a non-pedigree cat.

Finding A Kitten

Making The Choice

By far the majority of owners opt for a good, old-fashioned non-pedigree cat. They come in a wide variety of coat colours, and although most are generally short-haired, some may have semi-long or long coats. Some may be crosses between pedigree and non-pedigree cats, or even crosses between two different breeds – some new breeds such as the Burmilla, a cross between a Chinchilla and a Burmese, have been produced in this way. If you want more information about pedigree cats, you should purchase a book with information about particular breeds, or visit a cat show.

A litter of Persian kittens.

Many people acquire a new kitten via a friend or a relative who has decided to allow their own female cat to have a litter, and a kitten lovingly reared in a private home stands a good chance of making an excellent pet.

Rescue organisations also play a very important role in re-homing kittens.

What Age?

Some breeders insist on keeping kittens until they have completed their vaccination course at twelve weeks of age, but unless a kitten is coming into an environment where there is a particularly high risk of disease, I would recommend that kittens move to their new home as soon as they are fully weaned and independent from their mother. This is usually at seven or eight weeks.

Male Or Female?

Distinguishing the sex of kittens is not very difficult – but it is amazing how often people get it wrong. If you compare one kitten with another in the litter, it's even simpler – unless they are all the same sex!

A female kitten.

The female (queen) has a vertical slit-shaped genital opening just below the anus, whereas in the male (tom), the opening is round and spaced further apart. As the kitten matures, the testicles can be seen developing in the gap between the anus and the prepuce (the skin that covers the penis).

A male kitten.

Finding A Kitten

Signs Of A Healthy Kitten

Ideally, you should go and see a litter of kittens to observe how they behave together. The kitten you choose should be bold and alert, and unconcerned by the presence of a stranger. Do not be tempted to select the runt of the litter just because you feel sorry for it – you could be investing in future heartbreak.

Breathing:
Regular and even. Laboured breathing may indicate a respiratory infection.

Anus:
Soiling or soreness around the anus may indicate that the kitten is suffering from diarrhoea.

Abdomen:
A healthy kitten should not be excessively thin, but a swollen abdomen could be a sign of an illness such as a heavy worm infestation.

Skin:
A kitten should keep its coat well groomed. Look out for any parasites such as fleas, lice or mange mites.

Ears:
Clean and fresh-smelling. Abnormal discharge, foul smell, soreness, or signs of excessive irritation may indicate a problem.

Eyes:
Bright and clear. Look for signs of any discharge, and soreness of the conjunctiva surrounding the eye.

Nose:
Clean and free of discharge.

Mouth:
Look inside the mouth for any soreness of the gums or on the lining of the mouth itself.

It is best to purchase the equipment that you will require for your kitten before collecting it, to avoid any last minute panics. You don't need to splash out a great deal of money – often the simplest equipment is the best.

Carrier

Your first requirement will probably be for a carrier, so that you will be able to transport your kitten home safely and securely. Make sure you buy one that is large enough for an adult cat, or you will soon have to go to the expense of purchasing another. Don't buy a wicker basket, as this type often fails to fasten securely, and it is very difficult to clean if it becomes soiled.

Plastic carriers are the best type to choose. I is easier to get a cat in and out of the carrier if it opens at the top rather than the front.

However, some front-opening carriers have a quick-release catch around the side so that the top half can be easily lifted off. You can purchase synthetic fur bedding to line the carrier, although newspaper and a towel will be fine.

Make sure the carrier you buy will be big enough for an adult cat.

Cat Bed

Carriers that split into two halves can also be used as a bedding area for your kitten. This has the advantage of ensuring that your cat may not always run away and hide at the sight of the cat carrier, knowing that it invariably means a visit to the vet or the cattery.

There are some very attractive and entertaining cat beds available, in the shape of cars, telephone boxes and many other objects, but it is not worth investing a great deal of money in a cat bed since your kitten may well have its own views about exactly where it wants to sleep. A closed cardboard box, with a hole cut into it and some soft bedding inside, works perfectly well and can be thrown away when it gets soiled.

A cat carrier can be split so that it can also be used as a bed.

11

Be Prepared

Litter Tray

Another top priority is a litter tray because your kitten will not be able to go outdoors until after the vaccine course has been completed. Again, choose a tray of a reasonable size – it should be big enough to accommodate a growing kitten, but avoid a high rim otherwise your kitten will not be able to climb in.

Many owners prefer a tray with a covered lid, and many cats do seem to prefer the extra feeling of security that the roof provides.

Cat Litter

Obviously cat litter is an essential. The most widely available type is based on Fuller's Earth, and many now have deodorising agents added. It is important to keep the tray clean, or the kitten will refuse to use it. A litter-scoop can be used to remove soiled litter. Litter tray liners and disposable litter trays are now available to make the task easier.

Feeding Utensils

Feeding utensils do not need to be fancy.
Heavy porcelain bowls are better
than those made of plastic as they
are less likely to topple over and
can be more easily cleaned. You
will need one bowl for food and
one bowl for water – although
many cats do not drink a great deal,
fresh water should be available at all times. If
you feed a canned food, use a spoon that is kept
for animal foods only.

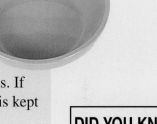

Comb

If you own a longhaired kitten, you should start
a grooming routine from day one, even if it is
not strictly necessary at that time. Families of
cats will groom each other as a form of social
bonding, and if you get your kitten used to the
experience from an early age it should remain
pleasurable for both cat and owner in later life.
Brushes have a tendency to skim over the
knots in the coat, and I find a fine-toothed
comb much more effective. Use the grooming
session as an opportunity to give your kitten a
regular check-
over (see
signs of a
healthy
kitten).

*Longhaired kittens, like
these Persians need
regular grooming.*

13

Be Prepared

Toys

There is a tendency for owners to overwhelm their kitten with toys, but often the simplest are the best. A kitten can have hours of fun with a table-tennis ball or an empty cotton-reel. Make sure anything you give is safe – for example, a kitten should not be allowed to chew and swallow wool.

Scratching Post

You will need to purchase a scratching post to keep claws in good order. Cat claws do not wear down like dog nails; they shed their outer skin to leave a new layer underneath. For this reason, I do not routinely recommend nail-clipping for cats.

Some cat toys and scratching posts are impregnated with catnip, a plant that seems very attractive to many cats. If your kitten is destined to remain an indoor cat, you may even want to invest in one of the elaborate 'cat-aerobic' centres, which are like indoor gymnasia for cats.

Collar

A collar is not a high priority while your kitten is being kept indoors, but a collar and tag is essential once he starts to venture outdoors. The collar must have either an elasticated section, or a quick-release that will open if pulled hard, to allow the kitten to escape if the collar gets snagged. The collar needs to be fastened tightly enough to stop it slipping off, but loosely enough to allow two fingers to fit under it. Check the fitting regularly to ensure it does not become too tight as the kitten grows.

The collar must have an elasticated section or a quick-release.

Cat-Flap

It is better to keep control of your kitten's comings and goings in the early days, but a cat-flap is very useful for older cats. Some are only operated if the cat wears a special magnetic collar to keep out unwanted visitors.

DID YOU KNOW?

'Kitty'', who lived in Croxton, Staffordshire, UK, gave birth to 218 kittens during her lifetime, with the last two being delivered at the age of thirty. She died just before her 32nd birthday.

Feeding Your Kitten

It is best to avoid any sudden changes in diet, especially for the first few days when your kitten is settling in. Try to find out what was being fed previously, and stick to it. Remember, kittens need to eat little and often.

Complete Diet

You should aim to feed a complete, balanced kitten food. It is much safer to feed a diet that has been specially formulated to contain all the nutrients that your growing kitten needs, rather than trying to produce a similar formulation from your own recipe.

Complete kitten foods can be either canned or dry. Although both are equally satisfactory nutritionally, in my opinion, it is cheaper and more convenient to feed a premium quality complete dry food, which can be left out for the kitten to eat ad lib during the course of the day. Canned food will go off more quickly, especially in warm weather, it is more messy, and works out more expensive on a like-for-like basis as the packaging is dearer.

Kittens seem to be able to cope with dry food from a surprisingly young age, but, if necessary, it can

A complete diet will provide for all your kitten's nutritional needs.

16

be softened with a little warm water or gravy. As the kitten grows into an adult, its nutritional needs will change, and it will need to be fed an adult rather than a kitten food. Later in life, your cat may need a food designed to prevent obesity in less active cats. Your veterinary surgeon should be happy to advise you about the diet that is best suited to your cat at any particular stage in its development.

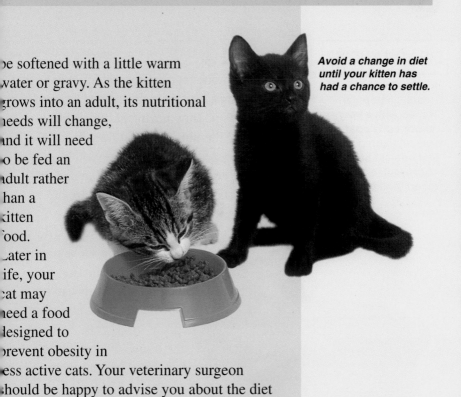

Avoid a change in diet until your kitten has had a chance to settle.

Traditional

Of course, you can feed a fresh meat-based diet if you wish, but it is important to give your kitten as wide a variety of foodstuffs as possible to prevent a deficiency from developing. Feeding a balanced mineral and vitamin supplement will also be helpful, but do not overdo the supplementation, as an excess can be harmful.

DID YOU KNOW?

The persecution of the cat in the Middle Ages allowed rats to multiply. Rat fleas carried Bubonic Plague, which in 1625 killed 35,000 people in London alone.

Feeding Your Kitten

Beware!

Cats are obligate carnivores, which means that unlike many other animals such as humans and even dogs, they have lost the ability to produce all the nutrients that they need from a vegetable-based diet. Therefore you must not try to feed your cat on a vegetarian diet, as severe problems such as heart failure or blindness can result.

However, many cats do seem enjoy chewing on vegetable matter from time to time. Since house-plants can be poisonous, it is advisable to grow some grass in a pot in the house if your kitten is a 'grass chewer' and lives mainly indoors.

Liquids

Fresh water must be available at all times, but there is no need for a kitten to drink milk. Small amounts may be fine, but an excessive amount will almost invariably cause digestive upsets. This is because kittens do not digest lactose (the sugar found in milk) very well, and it ferments in the bowel. Special cat milk with the lactose removed is available, and this can be given if your kitten is particularly keen on milk rather than water.

Training Your Kitten

Toilet Training

This is the first priority when your kitten arrives home. Position the litter tray where it is easily accessible, but also in a spot away from the main hustle and bustle. When you see your kitten sniffing around for a likely spot, particularly after mealtimes, you can pop him into the tray. Toilet training comes easily to kittens, but it is essential to keep the litter clean or the the kitten will not use it.

House Rules

Kittens are not like puppies, and few will learn to react to commands. However, you can you can start to lay down some 'house rules' from an early age. The best method of teaching is to give lots of encouragement, and positive reinforcement of good behaviour with rewards.

Occasionally you may need to punish your kitten for bad behaviour, such as chewing at electrical flex which can be very dangerous. Squirting a water-pistol or water-spray is quick and effective – your kitten will find it unpleasant, but it is not harmful. You have to catch the kitten 'red-handed' so that the kitten connects its misdeed with the punishment, and the kitten must not know that you have operated the spray, otherwise it will simply misbehave when you are not around.

Establish 'house rules' so your kitten learns what is permitted – and what is not!

Training Your Kitten

Using A Cat-Flap

At first, you kitten may be reticent about using a cat-flap and so it is important to give him confidence. The easiest way is to prop the flap open and tempt your kitten though with some tasty morsels. A transparent, perspex door is preferred by many cats.

With patience, your can teach your kitten to walk on a lead.

Lead Training

Some cats adapt to walking on a lead, but it is essential to start training at an early age. When your kitten is used to wearing a collar, attach a lead and allow him to wander where he chooses. It is best to do this in the house. When your kitten accepts the trailing lead, pick up the lead and, again, allow him to wander. Using treats, you can then encourage your kitten to walk with you. Keep training sessions short, and give lots of encouragement. Do not venture outside unti you are confident that your kitten is happy to walk on the lead.

Kitten Care

Most vets prefer a kitten to settle into its new home for a few days before starting the vaccination course, but if you wish, you can take your kitten for a health check immediately after purchase.

Vaccinations

It is advisable to vaccinate kittens against feline enteritis, cat flu and feline leukaemia virus, which are all potentially fatal viral diseases.

The vet can give your kitten a thorough health check when he goes for his vaccination.

The exact timing of the vaccinations depends upon the particular vaccine used, but, most commonly, the first injection is given at any time from nine weeks of age, and the second is given three weeks later. Sometimes a kitten may be a little off-colour for 24 hours or so after each injection, but very often they show no ill-effects at all.

The visits to the vet not only provide an opportunity for your kitten to receive a thorough health check, but also for you to obtain advice about any aspects of your kitten's care that may be concerning you. Your veterinary surgeon will probably discuss other aspects of preventative health care with you, as it is always best to take steps to prevent diseases from developing wherever possible rather than waiting for problems to arise.

Worming

If your kitten has not already been wormed, your vet will almost certainly advise treatment. There are two types of worms that commonly affect cats; roundworm, which look rather like fine lengths of thread, and tapeworm, which, as the name suggests, are much more flattened.

Roundworm are very common in kittens, as they are often passed on from their mother.

Tapeworm are much less common in kittens, a in order to live out their life cycle, they have to pass through an intermediate host such as fleas o wild animals that are eaten, so they take time to develop.

Fortunately, neither type of worm poses any significant threat to human health, but can affect the kitten's development if they are present in large numbers. In rare cases, a severe roundworm infestation can be fatal. Veterinary worming preparations are simple to use, safe and very effective, so there is no reason not to use them as a routine prevention on a regular basis.

Fleas

It is not unusual for kittens to bring some little six-legged visitors with them from their previous home, and even if there is no obvious sign of fleas, you should think about longterm flea prevention.

Life cycle: Fleas only live a small proportion of their life cycle on a cat. They lay several hundred eggs during their lifetime which drop off the cat and develop into larvae around

the home. Cat fleas are the commonest cause of skin disease in both cats and dogs, so taking preventative steps early on is well worthwhile.

Treatment: Insecticidal products can be quite toxic to young cats, so it is important to check the manufacturer's recommendations and ensure that the flea treatment you choose is suitable for kittens. Fortunately, several new veterinary products are now available that are both safe and effective in kittens.

If you know that your kitten has brought fleas into your house, you need to use a household product designed to stop fleas breeding around the home. In the short term, insecticides can be used to kill off adult fleas on your kitten. In the longer term, you can give your kitten a drug (taken orally in liquid form), once a month.

DID YOU KNOW?

A flea can jump about 118 times its own height. This is equivalent to a human jumping over a 60-storey building.

DID YOU KNOW?

All tortoiseshell cats are females, except in very rare cases where the cat has a disorder of the chromosomes.

Permanent ID

Permanent identification may be vital once your kitten starts to venture outdoors, as it is very common for young adults to get lost or injured. I have already mentioned the importance of an elasticated collar and identity tag, but it is all too easy for these to become separated from your cat. You should consider having your kitten permanently identified with a tiny microchip that can be injected under the skin of the scruff of the neck. This carries a unique number that can be read with a special scanner.

All the major rescue organisations now routinely scan cats that come into their care, and if a number is found, your details can be traced via a central computer.

Teeth Care

Dental problems are very common in older cats, but if you brush your kitten's teeth from an early age, you may prevent a lot of problems in later life. Cat dental kits are available for the purpose, with special enzymatic cat toothpaste and soft brushes. Feeding a dry cat food will also help to reduce the incidence of dental disease.

Going Away?

Don't forget to plan well ahead if you are going away. Avoid taking on a young kitten if you know you will be away from home in the near future. As kittens develop into young adults, they can be left alone at home for a few days if you have someone responsible who can come in at least twice a day for feeding and to check all is well.

Alternatively, you can arrange to board your cat, but a good cattery will be booked up well in advance during the peak holiday season. You will also need to provide an up-to-date certificate of vaccination.

If you brush your kitten's teeth from an early age, he will soon get used to the routine.

DID YOU KNOW?

It is very difficult to age a kitten accurately, except when they replace their baby canine teeth with adult ones at around five months of age.

Birth Control

Birth Control

If you have two kittens of different sexes, do not assume they will not mate with each other just because they are brother and sister. Young cats have no such scruples, and may sexually mature from about five and a half months of age. Most owners have their cats neutered before this age, unless a decision has been made to allow a female cat to have a litter.

Of course, if you own littermates of different sexes, you would not wish them to mate with each other, and you would need to have the male neutered. Given a free run out of doors, female cats will almost inevitably attract an entire tom cat and fall pregnant.

The Male

It is also important to neuter (i.e. remove the testicles of) males cats, not only to help in population control, but because entire tom cats will roam far afield, fighting viciously with other cats to try and establish as large a territory as possible. They also tend to mark their territory, and possibly your home, with their extremely pungent urine.

The Female

Do not let your cat have kittens for her sake – there are no health advantages, and the neutering operation (which will become necessary to stop her producing endless litters) is easier to carry out, and has less surgical risk, when she is about five months of age. The operation involves giving a general anaesthetic and making a small incision, usually on the flank, through which the ovaries and womb are removed.

Common Ailments

You should always consult your veterinary surgeon if your kitten seems unwell. A young cat does not have large energy reserves and so can deteriorate quickly if left untreated. This section outlines the more common diseases that affect kittens, and alerts you to the signs to look out for.

Cat flu

A common upper respiratory infection most often caused by one of two viruses. Signs may include sneezing, discharge from the eyes and nose, ulcers in the mouth, conjunctivitis and general lethargy and loss of appetite. Fortunately, vaccination has greatly reduced the incidence of this disease, but a kitten with a severe infection may require intensive nursing to survive.

Digestive Upsets

It is very common for a young kitten to get an upset stomach. Mild cases can be treated by withholding food for 24 hours and then giving a light diet such as boiled chicken and rice, little and often. If your kitten is vomiting repeatedly, passing blood, or if the problem does not settle down within a day or two, you should seek veterinary attention.

Feline infectious enteritis is a very serious viral infection that causes, among other signs, acute vomiting and diarrhoea. It is now quite rare, thanks to a very effective vaccine.

Common Ailments

Ear Mites

These are extremely common in young kittens, who are usually infected by their mothers. The tiny eight-legged animal lives down the ear canal and feeds on ear wax. The irritation that they cause stimulates the ear to produce a lot more dark wax. Any course of treatment must be continued for at least three weeks to kill off any eggs that may be present.

Feline Leukaemia Virus

This virus can cause a range of problems, affecting the immune system to bring about an AIDS-like disease, causing anaemia (a lack of red blood cells) or even cancer. There is nothing that can be done to kill the virus once infection has occurred, but a vaccine is available to help prevent it.

Feline Immunodeficiency Virus

This is another virus that causes an AIDS-like disease in cats, but fortunately neither are thought to be infectious to humans. It is transmitted mainly by biting and fighting, so is most common in young male cats. The signs that it can cause are very varied, but it is particularly associated with chronic gingivitis (inflamed gums).
Any kitten with general ill health that does not respond to treatment, or keeps

elapsing, should be blood tested for both feline
eukaemia virus and feline
nmunodeficiency virus.

Feline Infectious Peritonitis

Yet another viral disease that is common in
oung cats, although many cats that are
xposed to the virus that causes the problem do
ot go on to develop disease. It is particularly common in
ulti-cat households where there a lot of cats sharing
he same litter tray, which gives the infection a chance
o build up. In its most common form it causes an
ccumulation of fluid on the chest and abdomen, and is
ncurable.

Injuries

Curiosity often leads kittens into sticky situations, and
lthough they are generally pretty tough, broken bones, burns,
tings and other mishaps are not uncommon. Unfortunately,
ats are all too often the victim of road traffic accidents, and
n these cases, veterinary attention, sometimes over a long
eriod of time, may be necessary. Pet insurance is available in
nany countries and you may consider this to be a wise
nvestment.

Common Ailments

Skin Disease

Top of the hit list for skin parasites in kittens are definitely fleas, and even if you do not see the adults, you may see small, dark bits of flea-dirt on their bedding and in the coat (see Kitten Care – Fleas). Other parasites include lice, which live all their life cycle on the cat and stick their eggs to the hairs, and tiny fur mites, that live on the surface of the skin, causing irritation and excess scurf production. Ringworm is a fungal infection of the hair that causes bald, crusty patches to appear, especially around the head, and can be passed on to humans.

Toxoplasmosis

This single-celled parasite lives in the intestine of the cat, and only very rarely causes anything more that a mild diarrhoea. However, it is of some importance as it can cause harm to an immuno-suppressed human (e.g. someone receiving chemotherapy for cancer), or an unborn foetus if a pregnant women gets infected. For this reason, people in these categories should get another member of the family to clean out the litter tray regularly. It is thought that undercooked meat is a far more important source of infection in humans.

DID YOU KNOW?

Queen Victoria owned two blue Persian cats and did much to increase the popularity of pedigree cats.